salmonpoetry

Diverse Voices from Ireland and the World

the arts council
an chomhairle ealaíon
funding literature

Moonlight: A Full Moon

LOUISE C. CALLAGHAN

Published in 2022 by
Salmon Poetry
Cliffs of Moher, County Clare, Ireland
Website: www.salmonpoetry.com
Email: info@salmonpoetry.com

ISBN 978-1-912561-93-3

Cover Image: *Voyage, 1994* © Tim Goulding
Cover Design & Typesetting: *Siobhán Hutson*

Printed in Ireland by Sprint Print

*Salmon Poetry gratefully acknowledges the support of
The Arts Council / An Chomhairle Ealaíon*

For my friend, Susan Connolly

"Perhaps language, at least, possesses a belief in spirit."

Denise Riley

"Fear no more, says the heart, committing its burden to some sea, which sighs collectively for all sorrows, and renews, begins, collects, lets fall. And the body alone listens to the passing bee; the wave breaking; the dog barking, far away barking and barking."

Virginia Woolf, *Mrs Dalloway*

Contents

Corona

Murmurations

The Cretan Lyre

From forest to workbench: a carver
with a chisel chips and shaves away,
shaping hardwood cedar. Curls fly up
and fall to the floor. A lyraki fiddle
is all of a piece. Once carved it is hung
to dry and for the wood to darken.
A bow-maker chines a bow from
pernambuco. The lyre is threaded then
with three strings made of horsetail.
Ready now for the high melodies,
it is placed vertically on the knees,
longneck resting on the player's heart.
The first ripples of sound, our arms
and shoulders rise level: Zorba's Dance.
We start to move in a circle like trees.

Peeling Silver Birch

Strips of papery birch bark
flap thinly in the garden. Like

parchment on which to write,
print your ink-hieroglyphs —

a frieze, of bird, sphinx, bird…
until its trip-knots stop you.

Fluttering, scentless mystery,
an answer to my question.

Not, are you writing,
and, do you see the others?

But, are you dead lonely too?

August Harvest

Ich lieg allein im stillen Haus

Hermann Hesse

Stalks of the potato plant, yellowed,
wilted down before they ever flowered.
Bachelor that I am, each evening
I dig enough from the soft black clay,
seven or eight, for they are as small
as hen-laid eggs, to fill my cracked plate.

NOTE: The epigram is from Pearse Hutchinson's "Syllabics",
his small poem that delights in the solitary life.

Letter to My Sister

And I baked your cake with unusual care,
the Same Weight Cake: the weight
of three eggs matched with the same
of ground almond, sugar and butter.
Apricot halves, saffron-coloured,
pressed lightly in. The *Gleichschwer*,
you taught me to bake
there in your Burgau kitchen.

How should I not be glad? wrote Mahon.
I've decamped to my Garden Room,
wake to dill-scented air. You and I
share the same decade now, senior
citizens. Concerned for our family's
well-being. But what of the other
families, those who are homeless?
No summer camp, tennis, or sailing

for their children this Summer.
The migrants, and refugees who risk
their lives on the Mediterranean
for a life, a future here in our
increasingly inhospitable Europe.
Sert, on its perilous ocean edge
of Libya; Darfur, southern Syria.
Leaving homes which must be left.

Day begins in this frayed light,
a meadow of stars, beyond reach.
I'll take a dip later — full tide
immersion at Seapoint, a bouquet,
seaweed gathered breast-stroking
off wide steps of granite rock.
My birthday, how can I not be glad?
Clouds press close. Brightening later.

High Tide Late September

Walking the strand here in sunshine
the closer to happiness I've become:
thrum and pull of successive waves
onto the shore, seaweed-strewn sand,
the pleasure of all my senses, satisfied.
It doesn't seem to matter that my eye-
sight is dim or my hearing poor:
by the sea, a solitary with her thoughts.
Out on the surfed-water, a gull's cry.

*

Yet today I learnt of the sea's monstrous
and unpredictable ways. A swimmer,
bathing with countless others, enjoying
the swell of tide at the Forty Foot,
was brushed up against the rocks.
Another wave expanding, pulls him back.
With no ability to resist, the body
is thrust once more onto encrusted rock.
Onlookers, and rescuer, made irrelevant.

Murmuration of Starlings

for Maryrose & Colm

A flock wheels in the reddened sky, ripples and breaks
apart to form once more. At the point of dissolving
it is re-imagined as a falling wave, or a boat
steering the mackerel-clouded sky. Swarm-haze
suspended over a dome in the distance. On the turn
it gleams and flashes, silver steel. Starlings
are guided aerodynamically… in sevens:
between dusk and night stars here in Port Ortigia.
Beyond us then on the horizon. Nearly out of sight,
a calligrapher's calligraphy. Or held in the mind
as swathes of charcoal-black on the pitted paper,
a lithograph — across a West Cork winter hillside.

Three Waves

i. *Waves in Winter*

The sea spreads out silvery white
then rolls back into itself
over and over. We three

on the wall below the cliff,
count: every seventh wave
is stronger, has a longer life

before folding back.
The light, the air,
but most of all the deafening

sound of the sea forever
falling back into itself,
an ink-written, swirling surface.

ii.   *Waves, Mid–March*

Roused by wind and angry showers,
the heaving waves fold back
like howling lips.

We who witnessed them
crash in against the cliff
this Ides of March

read a glittering sleepless rage.

iii.   *Late Summer*

The push of waves onto the shore,
pulling out again as they withdraw.

Tide's small increments, half-rounds,
hours of call and response —

drawing stones and shells and shingle.
Until our long, our final exile.

On the Way to Santiago

empty of thought, and minds set free…
Susan Connolly

The pulse of the engine, the sleepy
atmosphere in the bus
as it speeds ahead into the dark

between one village and the next.

No small intimacy sitting so close
to someone who is bundled
beside you in half-sleep,

a factory worker, a night nurse…

Facing forward, we're all strangers,
except Birta, seated on the aisle
opposite me, her eyes shut.

Dawn, day seven of our pilgrimage,

we've sought a shortcut to Pontevedra.
For I am your lady, piped music
is cutting softly through

from the driver's radio. A song,

And I am your ma-a-an.
The response, deeper, more vibrato,
pulsing through me — part

physical, part spiritual. Mystical.

Winter in the Ruskin

for Mimi Khalvati

In off the wet street, through railings restored
after the war — two steps up and in at the door
of the old Ruskin Hotel, comes a bumble bee.

It bumps against glass of the foyer cubicle
catching the porter off guard, Hassan's not around.
I hear the cello-buzz as it goes on deeper

down dark corridors, insect legs dangling
like black empty suitcases, in at the stairwell,
now a cage-lift in the ancient, overheated hotel.

But the pollinator is far from lost, nor off course.
Obeying bee-laws, it will hole-up, slow down
enzymes or blood or whatever it does.

In its velvet vest, couch all through Winter,
nest in a vacant, subterranean mouse-hole.
The bee-heart, hibernate.

Landscapes, Cápri

Cápri — Regina of Rocks and Views,
dressed in April gowns of Amarynth
and Azucena*. As I go inhaling,
I unravel my joys and my desolation.

*

I see only misty scrub and a faint
grey horizon of sea-sky merge.
Bird-sounds erupt from a bush.
A solitary evergreen on the slope,
canopy of an Aleppo Pine.
A cock's high treble travels up

from Anacapri town. A girl
passes me on her mobile phone
wearing trainers and tracksuit:
Mamma, Mamma, ascolta.
A groan, almost human
of farm machinery from below.

*

My rocky climb has become
a woodland track opening onto
a meadow dotted with daisies
and pale scentless violets.
A tiny green lizard scurries
from green to green.

When your eyesight fails,
name what is close at hand,
small things hidden in the grass.
Along the mud-path leading
to the Hermitage, in its shadow
on a wrought-iron plaque

Rilke's lyric, *Tramonto, Cápri*,
his cry: listen, listen my heart.

* "Cápri Reina De Roca/En Tu Vestido/De Color
Amaranto Y Azucena/ Viví Desarrollando/La
Dicha Y El Dolor…" Pablo Neruda

Blackbird Hello

The old year lingers too long.
Oh blackbird, where are you?

I need your solitary song.
Sing out your three notes.

But it is starlings' whoosh
that ushers brightening dawn.

And on the radio, on the hour,
Couperin's baroque guitar.

Les Deux Tours, Marrakech

Early morning, then again at evening,
I listen for the purr of turtle doves,
a throated ripple from the *Palmeraie*
 Water Garden.

Compared to the wren, or sparrow:
rusty mechanics of a wheelbarrow,
all Winter back home, to and fro,
 to and fro.

Winter Landscape, with Moorhens

Bare-leaf trees, head-first
in the still water of the canal.
From the bank, a moorhen
breaking its mirror…

On the bridge, I stare deeply
until I see stars rather than debris,
golden granules of light
on the shuffled surface.

Streets, grown quiet before
the under-rumble arrival
of my Luas tram. A warm
exhale from its sliding doors.

Kilnamona Chronicle

The Red Wool Coats

The two little girls, wrapped in winter coats,
their mufflers looped round their necks,
were sent outside to play. The Babies,
they were always called in those days.

As they crossed the yard, passing the stables
and run-down outhouses where kittens
were often born, and the empty car port,
their plan unfolded without a word being spoken.

Around the front, the house, all eyes
with its nine windows, they undressed.
Despite the cold they removed their knickers
and their bainín-wool coats.

After easing the warm, elasticated knickers
down over their flattened fringes to cup
their heads, they buttoned each other up
into the back-to-front red coats.

Draughts of cold air on their legs and buttocks,
their bare bottoms, didn't bother them
in the least — their faces, alight as they sang
and shrieked abuse at the wind:

you bloody, bloody… bloody, bloody!
knowing full well, later there'd be trouble.
This is how I remember it anyway —
once outdoors, our defiant glee.

Do You Remember?

Do you remember the times we knelt up
on the back seat — travelling backwards
all the way home from St Matthias,
our little one-room school in Ballybrack?

Your mother was doing the home-run.
We viewed Tryrrell's fields rushing by
as she drove over Harnie's Bump,
and the trickle of river, the Shanganagh.

We couldn't read that name painted
on the Marble Works gate, nor knew
that *Hayes & Sons* meant those who hewed
markers for the dead. Since I lived further,

closer to the village, we engined on
past the wall of your house. Your mother
stopped to drop me off. I peeled my knees
off the leather seat and climbed down

from her shuddering motor, piping out
goodbye-and-thank-you-very-much.
I skipped in at the side-gate, happy
that I'd see you again tomorrow.

To this Summer day, I don't know
the tall walls, you have lived behind
and continue to live behind: a Home
or Asylum, since you were seventeen —

but I long to invite you into my memories.

Coming Home from School

The granite stone wall — old grandeur
surrounding a former estate, Athgoe —
on the way home on my own from school.

A nook, a small cranny at pocket-level,
begging for treasures. Under my hand
I feel a rubble of pebbles and fallen grout.

In the hollow, a glass marble, the stub
of an ordinary pencil, and a farthing.
Now I place a silver thruppenny-bit.

Here every little thing would keep forever.

Kilnamona Chronicle

i

You always loved dogs, I loved kittens best,
any kitten, among litters born twice a year.

I wheeled them round the yard in our sister's
old doll's pram. Pocketing bits of sausage

from the tea table, I'd sneak out in the dark
to their nest in the stables, bring them scraps.

By then you'd your own dog, a cocker spaniel.
I must have been five, for you were nearly ten.

ii

You never knew, your spaniel had pups
which were half-mongrel. How the local dog,

Sparky, from nearby Eaton Brae estate,
was glued to her for half an afternoon.

Our efforts to separate them, Paddy & I,
were fruitless, first on the front lawn

where we grappled with them and then
in the flower bed, among Mum's roses.

You were away in boarding school and no one
wanted to disillusion you. Not in a letter.

Dismantling the Crib

i.

Up rummaging in her dressing-room,
buried beneath the silken slips
and folded underwear, I discover
the figure of the infant Jesus,

an array of four plaster angels
and Mary and old St Joseph.
In years to come, it's where I'd go
for my supply of sanitary towels.

ii.

Up on the cold, unlit altar,
the oldest nun of the Community,
her black habit and hand-knit mittens,
is kneeling to divest the Crib.

The same day the Wise Men set out
East for home, and we boarders
return, Mother Francis, once more
boxes away the Holy Family.

She wraps individually each papier-
maché sheep and each little lamb.
Lastly, she swaddles the Baby Jesus
in snowy tufts of cotton wool…

The simplicity of a myth that has
sustained her solitary life. At Mass
next morning, beeswax and incense
welcomed us young girls back to school.

The Little Housemaid

Her feet were filthy, her legs,
streaked with unnameable dirt.
The girl from the orphanage
fascinated me: her black eyes

under her black fringe. And her
expression of such insolence
as she bobbed a curtsey
to my grandmother. As if to say

what does she want now!
Her yes, ma'am sounded to me
more like yes-mum.
Yes-mum this, yes-mum that.

Skin so pale, she might never
have seen the sun — there
in the Manor, her quarters
in the cold kitchenette.

She'd eat you out of house
and home, that one, murmured
Granny to my mother.
Words, I easily overheard.

Along wood-panelled passages,
in her black canvas shoes,
she'd no bother giving me the slip
in our games of hide and seek.

Bettystown

A still bay where little waves
have given up their shells

to paddle-shallows, or
lodged in ripple-chevron Vs

of firm sand. The razor-
shell, ear-pink and harmless

until the one you stepped on,
runner — hard, heavy, heel-first.

Highway to Rome '64

And our bus sped on towards
the Eternal City.
As we neared its tawdry outskirts

kneeling up on the back seat —
a sight whose beauty
I would never forget.

On a fast, horse-driven cart,
a woman, bare-breasted
feeding her newborn child.

Splendour, on dusty boards,
in the folds of her clothes,
cradled in her arms.

Prayer of her whole body.

The Diplomat's Daughter

The Summers of Hesperides are long.
E. Dickinson

i

She arrived late, just as we'd settled in
to the boredom of a new school year.
Already absorbed into Form Four
were the new Day Girls, wearing
their too long uniform wool-skirts.

Mother Trinita appeared with her
before Break, interrupted History
to present this little dark-haired girl
at her black-garbed side.
Michèle was dressed in a tartan kilt

which met navy knee-length socks
and a sky-blue twinset. Most enviable,
her moccasin slip-on shoes.
Everything she wore fitted to perfection.
When faced by us twelve-year olds

she wasn't shy at all. Breaktime, we vied
to carry her across the muddy pitch
on our sedan of interlocked hands
and wrists. Our storybook princess
happily played along.

Later I learned, this arrangement
was to allow her father time
with his new wife — untroubled,
you'd imagine, by a clever,
too pretty daughter.

ii

Mother Wolstan, a tiny wrinkle-faced nun,
the Infirmarian, might be your first
port of call if you were feeling unwell.
A kind smile, a pat on the arm,
solace enough for a homesick child.

And maybe she sought Mother Immaculata
in the Old Building, to apply for stamps,
or sanitary towels from her store
in the windowless stockroom.
The Old Building — domain of the nuns,

where we assumed they ate and
slept, or wrote letters home.
Evenings spent listening to programmes
on the radio. Whether old or young,
it was impossible for us

to comprehend that they were women.
We slept apart, in small dormitories
in the new block. Our curtained cubicles,
just space enough for a narrow-frame
bed and a personal locker.

She confided in me one night, whispered
to come into her veiled cubicle,
held the blankets open to let me in.
She related in small sobs some disaster
of Christmas, the holidays at home

where she felt unwanted. She asked me
to hold her, but I withheld myself,
afraid to comfort her, afraid
of being caught — our convent
school that policed touch.

iii

Trinita beat her once. On her upper legs,
her buttocks. Vivid bruises, splinters
of blood breaking through the skin.
Typical of her, to tell and show
the dramatic result of this assault.

Refusing shame, she turned the blame
where it belonged, to the nun,
unaccountable to anyone, *in loco parentis…*
Some ungoverned passion of her own?
By now, we were reading Exodus,

shared a single copy by tearing
the paperback three ways. Then we tore
Gone With the Wind. We never
lowered ourselves to reading Angelique,
or day-girl fodder of a Georgette Heyer.

Between classes, head-holding the lid
of my desk open, I devoured a page more
of Memoirs of a Dutiful Daughter.
My de Beauvoir was one book
I couldn't bear to share.

We read Dr Zhivago, in hardback.
Michèle, quoting Pasternak's
Zhivago poem, Hamlet, in her essay:
Life is not a walk across a field — aware
somehow of the unfathomable future.

Summer nights, at an upstairs window
overlooking the bay,
we watched couples, in parked cars,
bundled in the back seat.
Through cedars, the contours of Bray Head.

The Late Sixties

Ducts and struts and huge joints
that are called gerberettes —
with its services all on show.
In sunshine, bolts of silver light.
Exterior trumpets, loudly colourful
like open mouths. They sang to us,
him and I that summer day, Paris
at the Pompidou, two students,
passing through.
             A year later,
on the overnight ferry to Crete,
because of the heat, we slept on deck.
We settled in beside the funnel —
like those Pompidou trumpets
that conducted indoor air out.
Never so alone as when I woke
in a river, the funnel's vapour,
blackest night, in a foreign dark.

Mother & Baby

Sometimes she's been driven to imagining
she gave birth to him all right — her son,
but then was tricked into giving him away.

In the Home for mothers, unmarried girls,
in the Midlands, on the edge
of a town — in case word gets out.

Come on now, says Matron, push down
hard. She finds the sunken eyes of the nun
as the baby gushes between her thighs.

Into a fragile Winter afternoon, thin cries,
the high-ceilinged room. He'd be taken then.
She, more betrayed than betraying.

This child, to whom she'd given a secret name
in her mind — he'll come looking for her
one day, longing to find out who she is.

Corona

In Our Isolation

to Oisín, Oscar, Luke & Jack

The whispering dry leaves
dark-cornered in my garden

remind me of teenagers,
the boys that caught my eye

on street-ends, in sunlit alleys,
the Friday schools closed.

In threes and fours,
before the virus took hold.

No heed of risk, nor
the distance they might observe.

Then, like leaves I swept away,
no further liberty.

Pandemic Rounds

i.m. Dr Li Wenliang, Wuhan

Day 1

Displacing a blackbird
with her footfall

there she goes
round the garden,

a toe-heel jogging
the longest way

possible around
its small perimeter.

She counts the thirty-
second circles —

finding a rhythm
is all important.

Past an Exochorda,
and a Hebe,

under the arch,
stretched with briars

of an Albertine rose.
Her laps, a virtual

assault course.
She traverses slabs

of the patio, rounding
a wrought-iron table,

two garden chairs.
Trying not to fall.

Pandemic Rounds

Jogging the A4 page
of her small garden
is her way of looking
and marking a rhythm
to these strange new days.

Past over-blown tulips,
a straggle of daffodils,
gone-to-seed celandines.
And the faded green
petals of a Christmas Rose.

April Solo

the pale day appears…
Pablo Neruda

When I open the curtains,
my darkened room
starts its talk with the day,
joins the conversation
of garden birds.

My eye follows a flight-
path froth–blossoming
over the sky, voluble
yet silent. And I think of you
up too, the same hour,

at your bedroom window,
the waning moon…
By the time I write,
the pilot is half-way
across our quietened world.

My Stepping Stones

to Susan

The granite discs
        set in grass,
                child-hopping
                        distance apart,
                            are the ribs
                    of my garden.
                Placed just so,
                        like a good verb
                                making a sentence
                                    strong.

Her Concrete Poems

Her poems
        like a pram
                full of kittens

                        down the North Road,
                                on her way
                                        to Angela Greene's.

                And as hard to place
in a good home.

Easter Rain

after Du Fu (709-770)

Outside the city
in each small garden

white blossoms rain,
grieve our isolation.

They scatter, then gather
in wastes and gullies.

Time closes in on me,
I have achieved nothing,

says the poet, Du Fu.

My Fowl

Preening their red feathers,
they puff out the fluffy
silver under-down.

In the enclosure
of the hen-run they wallow
in hollowed dust-bowls

and then rigorously
shake themselves free,
in showers of dust,

of mites and fleas.
Of the three it is Sylvia
who's my favourite.

Corona

i.m. Abhishek Jain (New Delhi), April 25th, 2020

I shall relight my fires
come this Friday — May 1st:
make the sign of the cross
over milk, over buttermilk,
mark the oven-ready bread loaf.
Like every able-bodied person

I'll apply the sweeping brush
to the kitchen floor. Dust
and mop. I'll wash my hair,
let it dry in the open air.
But first I'll place this crown

on the gate-rail, blossoms
of every flower I can find,
to mourn those who have died.
Him, her, dearest to someone,
someone I may know. Aware
that this time I have been spared.

Call & Response

i.m. Eavan Boland, Dublin, April 27th, 2020

A constant call and response
of two blackbirds since dawn.

Since dawn, her body laid out
in its grave-clothes,

in folds of a linen shroud.
Her palest mother-skin…

The air outside is a cascade
of falling blossom.

And my enduring lilac tree,
crowned with buds of lilac.

A radiance that is this day,
May Day, yet is painful.

Memories, our only answer
in response to her death.

Cartography & Music:
Inis Meáin

Eyes no longer as keen for detail,
I hear the concertina,
a polka, jig, some kind of reel –
it fades and then flowers again.

Somewhere up there on the hillside
between here and Cill Ceannanach,
depending on the breeze, the music
reaches over to the Old Harbour pier

to us that have ears to hear.
A donkey, an orange pony,
each in its tiny rock-defined field,
a one-horned bull, his harem of three.

To the flock of speckled starlings,
lined like musical notation
along the telegraph wires;
for here there are no trees.

And over towards Vilma Conneely's
where she is taking her ease,
on Zoom with her daughter.
Its gaita-like, reed music.

And to Dara Beag, who found
the map of his whole life here,
now his death, Samhain 2012,
at rest in Rialaig Cemetery.

Gulls echoing over the Sound
catch the melodeon-note
as it falls, and the campanula bells
and all of August flora…

A rook or tortoiseshell butterfly
are more likely to find its source
than I, walking to the shore,
on the seaweed-scented air.

The lie of the island, every named
field, every rock and stone
is gathered in the eye of its music.
Amid the uncertainty, our compass-rose.

Note: Tim Robinson, cartographer of Inis Meáin,
died during the Covid 19 Pandemic, April 2020.

Concertina Player

On the hill, at her open door,
a chair on the concrete step,

she plays a small ornate box
rested lightly on her knee.

In the sunshine she practises
all afternoon, moving

from tune to tune:
a waltz, the slow airs

that rise and fall
into grikes and fissures,

over sun-warmed tablerock
where her listener walks.

A Farewell

Air captured in the small box
is blown along the reeds.

Push and pull… a gasp,
then pressed again.

From its modulated throat
the freed notes spill

far and near. A plaintive
quavering tune.

In the months to come,
that Summer noon

will leave an after-echo
vibrating in your mind —

its hum, a comfort
you'll carry with your grief.

A Rage for Order

i.m. Derek Mahon, 2nd October 2020

The line, whether long or short,
the word on the page,
the sounds that surround it,
your final image. A storm

where you become warmer,
closer to finding the words.
And the poem that is forged,
is your rage for order.

A Field Below the Woods

The ditches are cut back,
the low-growing hazel hacked
and the blackberry briars
laden with their black jam fruit.

The ditches are cut back
to open a clearance, inhospitable
to the make-shift tent,
a solitary old woman who slept

Winter long in it. Empty
battered beer cans remain.
But what of that! A casual
desecration of the verge.

The margins of a field,
like the annotated margin —
a poem, even land-deal,
on our page-a-day Book of Kells.

A Journey

All these words
are as linked to my body,
every nameable part,
as the ink to the page
that I write.
Isolate, sensory, intimate.

Beyond Myself

The pages of my life
read on and on
to my final breaths.
Eyes first, exhausted stars,
until I leave behind
only echoes. No more world.

Unforseeable

My skin shivers: No more seagulls
over the rooftop   at sleepless dawn.
Nor apple windfalls drop dead weight
on furrowed grass. Unforeseeable
suffering before   these wonders
of time and space   for me are shut.

Heron

for Marion Roche

'He is all wings and no fuselage and probably hollow inside…'*
is not how I see the heron.
Ours, a delicate silver-grey
presence at the end of the Pier,
instructing fishermen here
to stillness and us walkers
to patience, calm. Watchful
in this end-year light,
every muscle ready for flight.
And later inland, at dawn,
from the river, bare trees,
the unearthly screech –
I see it through closed eyes:
tongue of a new moon,
first hint of guillotined night.

* Francis Harvey

Prayer for Bridget's Day

for Gaye

Liminal places where
rest and peace reside,
places that inspire you,
where the divine
seems to be present…
In Spring snow-light,
remind yourself
when you are tired,
to go there: there
among the folds of its
dream-world, find
understanding, clarity.

Diamond Rocks Ceremonial

Pinks, thrift and clouds of white clover
shimmer on an edge of the cliff.
Inching closer, the deep sighs
of waves, breathing far below.
Out on Moore Bay, cut off
somehow, a grass-capped island,
field for half a cow.

These rocks I've walked across
are table-wide, pocked with silver
and saffron-coloured lichens.
I step the cracks carefully.

Children with fluorescent nets
are searching shallow rock-pools,
they lean in alert for any movement.
Limpets, sea-urchin, suckered
to the rocks, and periwinkles.
Pale transparency of a shrimp
that darts for cover, until a sharp
wind shimmers the water shut
like a camera lens.

Rocks, shot with mineral diamond,
a colourless lustre. On the horizon,
halo-blaze of the setting sun.

Winter Wonders

We stood there crouched down
in a fold of the front stairs
and gazed, not so much in awe
as trying to work it all out,
how human, angel, animal fit
together – the rustic cedar hut.
Three kings, like cousins of ours
we'd see only once a year,
Drinks on Christmas morning.
But the stair made room for mystery.

I can imagine the mist rising
off wet grass, and shepherds,
(lads like the butcher's three sons)
their excited sense of purpose
arriving at the backyard shed,
the breathing beasts, manure scent
instead of frankincense or myrrh.
My picture-book store of memory
these darkest days, an easement
to this enduring uncertainty.

Acknowledgements

Grateful thanks are due to the editors of the following publications in which some of these poems first appeared.

Poetry Ireland Review 126, editor, Eavan Boland
Cyphers 89 and 92. editor, Eiléan Ní Chuilleanáin
The Irish Times 15/2/20, editor, Gerard Smyth

I would like to thank Tim Goulding for his cover artwork, *Voyage*.

Thanks to Thomas McCarthy for his enthusiasm and generous reading of my work over many years.

Thanks to Manchán Magan for reading and responding to these and earlier poems.

Thank you to John Fanagan, for proofreading – and for his invaluable knowledge of English usage.

My thanks to Gaye Polacsek and Patricia Skar.

I would like to thank Susan Connolly for her support in writing this collection. Most of all, I am grateful for her friendship and our sharing of poetry, over thirty years.

LOUISE C. CALLAGHAN was born in Dublin, Ireland in 1948. She is the author of *The Puzzle-Heart* (1999); *Remember the Birds* (2005); *In the Ninth House* (2011) and *Dreampaths of a Runaway* in 2017. She is editor of an anthology of poetry called *Forgotten Light: Memory Poems* (A&A Farmar, 2003). Her poems have been published in journals throughout Ireland and the UK and are included in *The Field Day Anthology of Irish Literature*, Volumes IV & V, Voices and Poetry of Ireland (Cork University Press), and *Windharp: Poems of Ireland Since 1916* (Penguin Books, 2016). Her work is recorded in the Irish Poetry Reading Archive, UCD. Her play, *Find the Lady*, which is based on the life of Kate O'Brien, was commissioned by the Abbey Theatre Company in 1993. Louise has taught creative writing in Ireland and the US. She has an M.Litt in poetry from St Andrews, Scotland (2007). *Moonlight: A Full Moon* is her fifth collection of poems with Salmon Poetry.

salmonpoetry

Cliffs of Moher, County Clare, Ireland

"Publishing the finest Irish and international literature."
Michael D. Higgins, President of Ireland